SCRIBE PHARISEE AND THE LAMB OF GOD

MAN MUST ACCEPT A LOVING GOD HE CAN NEVER UNDERSTAND

FLOYD YELTON

authorHOUSE®

AuthorHouse™
1663 Liberty Drive
Bloomington, IN 47403
www.authorhouse.com
Phone: 1-800-839-8640

Published by AuthorHouse   03/12/2012

ISBN: 978-1-4490-5618-6 (sc)
ISBN: 978-1-4490-5619-3 (e)

Library of Congress Control Number: 2010905727

This book is printed on acid-free paper.

IN MEMORY OF

Andrew and Undean Yelton

We chose God, We worked for Him.
We chose the ministry, We worked for Him.
We chose birth, We worked for them.
We chose the church, We worked for them.

We answered God's call, We worked for all.
We now work in another room.

By Floyd Yelton Scribe and Pharisee

And

The Beautiful Souls God and I Love

Table of Contents

Introduction

I have always believed in God and was even curious enough to look forward to some day finding out just what God was. I was unable to accept Christ as the Son of God. He was at best a good man who lived a life I could never live. The most difficult thing in my life has been to accept that something as simple as believing in Christ could ever make a difference in me. I reasoned that something so simple could not be the way of a God who could create all I could see or know. I reasoned that, if God existed and represented good; you would have to live the life of Christ. I reasoned that if God had a plan it must be clear to all, not as confusing as Christianity. I reasoned....

One day I sat on a bench waiting to catch a train and had a very simple thought. That thought was that it was time to for me to stop reasoning and accept that Christ was indeed real. In the middle of that thought, before the thought ended I experienced the presence of God. It is and will always be impossible to understand what and why it happened. There is so much difference between God's presence in me and my presence. These poems are an attempt at describing that, which **cannot be understood, explained, described, justified or reasoned**.

From now to forever God let me live.

From now to forever God let me live. for today let me
be Healthy.
From now to forever God let me live. for today let me
be Wealthy.
From now to forever God let me live. for today let me
be Wise.
From now to forever God let me be wise. for today be
with those I love.

God believes in Me

God exists for me,
God is real not belief,
I love my neighbor,
I love God,
because God believes in me.
I can face life's problems,
I can face the unknown,
I can resist my self,
I can face my death,
because God has faith in me.

My simple belief is answered with God' s presence
God believes in ME !
God has faith in ME !

1

God does not exist in these words.

God does not exist in my faith,
nor my words.
God does not exist in your faith,
nor in your words.
God does not exist in the faith,
nor in the words of others.
If you are to know God.
He will exist in *your* heart,
your mind and *your* soul.
God awaits *your* decision.

I pray that the presence of God be yours.

God exists in you and me

God is not in the Church or Choir.
God is not in the book or word.
God in not is the sky or the stream
God in not in furry little animals

God exists in you and me.

God Gives Life

God gives life with options.
Each life must choose life each Day.
Each life must choose life after death.
God gives life forever.

God has made me Speechless

God has given me joy I cannot describe.
God has given me knowledge I cannot explain.
God has given me truth I cannot understand.
God has given me love I cannot earn.
God has given me life I never had before

God is the answer

When the joy of life overflows
God is the answer
When the sorrow of life comes
God is the answer
When the abundance of life comes
God is the answer
When the famine of life comes.
God is the answer

God Spoke to ME

As surely as God spoke to Adam,
God spoke to me.
As surely as God spoke to Abraham,
God spoke to me.
As surely as God spoke to Jesus,
God spoke to me.
As surely as God spoke through Christ,
God spoke to me.
As surely as God spoke to me,
God will speak to you.
Listen

Life and more Abundant

The Greatest Joy is being in the presence of God
and not being afraid.
The Greatest Mystery is how God could love me so much.
The Greatest love is God's presence for me.
The Greatest Absolute is God's presence.

The Greatest Joy grows.
The Greatest Mystery broadens.
The Greatest Love deepens.
The Absolute remains

Belief

I believe in Christ.
God comes to me.
God believes in me!

God's Grace

My faith is human, it cannot withstand all.
It is not my faith in God,
It is Gods faith in me that gives me life.
My beliefs cannot change reality.
It is not my belief in God
It is God's belief in me that changes me.
My mind can ask questions I cannot answer.
When the whys seem to overpower me.
God's presence makes the whys unimportant.
It is God, who changes me,
not I who changes God.

God's Love

Christ has already come
when you have God's love.
God has already judged
when you have God's love.
Death is a door not the end
when you have God's love.
The end of time has come.
when you have God's love.

God's nature

God could have created the world,
God could have created the stars,
God could have created heaven,
God could have created me,
does it really matter?

I exist, God loves me.

I endure

When my logic fails me, God Endures.
When my hope fails me, God Endures
When my wisdom fails me, God Endures.
When my faith fails me, God Endures
When my body fails me, I will Endure

I love you

I love God as he loves me.
His presence insures compliance.
I love you as God commands me.
His presence insures compliance.

I love you more because
by your choice
God lives in you.

GOD

exists even if I can not see God;
is known even if I will never understand God;
loves me even if I will never deserve such love;
softens me even if I am hardened;
speaks to me even if sometimes I am deft;
knows me even if I am unknowing;
He lives in me. Even though, I am not God;
God has done all this through Jesus.
God has done all this by his presence and love.
I am reminded of all this through you.
You are a distributor of God's Love.

Mans Secret Prayer BC

A cave man warmed by fire uttered God,
and a worshiper lights a candle.
He looked beyond at the darkness,
and the preacher shouts Work of the Devil.
O God, if you exist and have a plan for mortals.
Forgive me if I light a candle.
I can neither escape my afterbirth nor live in darkness.

Mans Secret Prayer AD

May life's greatest be yours.
Life's greatest joy
Life's greatest mystery.
Life's greatest love.
Life's greatest absolute.
May the presence of God be yours.
Escape your afterbirth and live in light.

My Song, My Sermon, My Prayer

God is greater than the Church, Pray for me, Pray for me.

God is greater than the Church, Pray for me, Pray for me.

God is greater than the Bible, Pray for me, Pray for me.

God is greater than Jesus, Prayer for me, Pray for me.

God is greater than God, Pray for me, Prayer for Me

God is the only absolute, I pray for You, I pray for you.

With your belief, God speaks without sound.
God's presence fills the heart, the mind the soul.

With your belief, God speaks without sound.
God's presence fills the heart, the mind the soul

With your belief, God speaks without sound.
God's presence fills the heart, the mind the soul

Everything

Everything else is momentary
Everything else is transient
Everything else is less
when you have God's love.

Revelations

If God gave me free choice.
My future has not been written.
With God's love
The future will be with God.
With God.
The future will be good.

God's Failures

God is great but could be greater.
He could have eliminated my pain.
He could have made me smarter.
He could have made me better
He could have made me God.

When you are human it is all too easy to be God.

Why

I can ask questions I cannot answer
I can know things I cannot explain
I can experience things I cannot understand
God made me human not God

Thank You God

God Is

God cannot be judged by fate.
God cannot be judged by the action of believers.
God cannot be judged.
God is not belief.
God is.

Questions and Answers

God created me to ask questions I cannot answer.
It must be the effort not the results, which is important.
It must be the trip, not the destination.
It must be the question, not the answer.
God lives in me.
It must be the results not the effort that is important.
It must be the destination, not the trip.
It must be the answer, not the question.

It is for God not me.
It is human for me to try.

Search for God

Search for God in the book,
in the word,
in others.
When you find God.
Revealed by a mustard seed of acceptance.
It will be in you.
Where he was all along.

Everything else pales

In the belly of a whale.
In the arms of a mob.
In the embrace of cancer.

God loves you.

Everything else is faith.
Everything else passes.
Everything else pales.

God Gives All

It is not the quality,
the intensity or the amount of your faith.
Faith does not make you smarter,
make you wiser or,
allows you to understand God.
Faith does not reveal God's mysteries,
his methods or the future.
Faith does not change your heart,
your mind, or your soul.

It is the simple acceptance of Christ and God.
God's faith in you gave and gives all.

As I Judge, I will be Judged

I will not judge those I do not know.
I will not judge those I do not understand.
I will not judge those whose shoes I have not walked in.
I will not judge those who violate Gods law.
I will not be judged.
but
I must judge my actions.
I must judge my thoughts.
I must judge my heart.
I must judge all.
Without judgement there
is no difference
In Man and Beast.
Without judgement there
is no difference
In God and Man.

The Small Step to God

Forgive me God.
Thank you God.
Be with me always.
So that my last step is the
The Small step to You.

Millstones of Faith

Believers and especially the yet to believe

God is understood
by the young of heart the
simple of mind and
the trusting soul.

The millstones are:

Maturing at the expense of a young heart.
Knowing at the expense of the mind.
Worship at the expense of the spirit.
Loving mankind at the expense of man.
Loving the messenger at the expense of the message.

Mountains of Faith in a Sea of Amen's

God

Known but not Understood.
Present but not Seen.
Absolute but not definable.
The mountain moved by a mustard seed.

Christ Taught

Christ taught
Love God
Love your neighbor
Abundant Life
and through me to God.
How can man clarify that with
so many words and so many Faiths.

God - Man – Beast

If all men are equal,
there is no difference in
Good and Evil.
If all men are equal,
there is no difference in
God, Man or Beast.
All men are equal,
All men are
God, Man and Beast.
All men are not alike
Some accept Christ
and with the heart and mind
nurture the God within.

Some Days

Hope is lost,
The heart aches,
The world is sad.

Judgement is rendered,
forgiveness is sought,
life is restored.

Loves smothers,
The soul soars,
the world is beautiful.

God's Will

God's will is not the faith of others.
God's will is not your faith.
God's will is available from God
A mustard seed that accepts Christ.
God reveals his will.
God's will is love and be loved.

Love

God's presence
God's grace
God's will
God

I Know

I believe:
that I can dream;
that I can imagine;
that I can create;
I know
that God reveals.

I believe;
that which I read;
that which I learn;
that which I accept;
I know
that which God reveals.

I Trust

I do not need to know
What, when, where.

I trust God

I would like to know
What, when, where.

God's Choice

God believes in me.
I cannot know the future.
I am unable to speak for God.
I am thankful each day.
God chooses to be with me,
each day God has faith in me.

Forgive me God

I can feel
I can imagine
I can think
I can trust
I can know

Things only you could know.

God Trades

God trades without measure;
Mountain for a mustard seed;
Eternity for a thought;
Your love for his love;
Life for death.
God gets you
Paul for Saul

God trades for You

God is not a Supreme Human
is not a super Dad
a unquestioning Love
an all knowing Being
a fair Judge
God's is greater than that

God trades for You

I Know Too

I know I am right when
God presence lingers.
I know I am wrong when
God presence fades.

I know.

I am

Christ was and is.
God is and was.
I am and will be.

The meal so great it overflows

God knows me well
I do not have to tell him he is great
to ask for forgiveness
to worship him
the meal offered, is consumed within
the filled soul, must be shared

Man's words and thoughts

Water, wine, bread, and light
all of man's words cannot describe God
almighty, great, joy and hope
all of man's words cannot describe God' love
rock, foundation, pillar and everlasting
and still they fall short.
all of mans words cannot describe God.
all of man's thoughts can not reveal God.

Peace

I am as amazed as you
The door I opened is not closed to you
The meals I receive are not at your expense
The life I have can be yours as well
You
Must open the door
Accept the meal

Peace

There may be other doors
other paths
other meals
that lead to God.
I only vouch for my mine.

When two or more

If two Christians believe, if a million Christians believe,
if a million churches believe, is God revealed?

If two Christians think, if a million Christians
think,
if a million churches think, is God bound?

If you accept Christ,

God reveals himself.
God binds himself.

Spirit to Spirit

Revealed and Bound
God speaks without sound
Embraces without touch
Is seen without sight
Known but not understood
Your Faith is converted to the Absolute

God's Love

God's presence is love, love is God's presence
God's love can not be enhanced by man's faith
God's love can not be enhanced by man's actions
Man's faith and actions only dilute God's love.
God's love can only be shared.

God reveals God

God is mirrored in Christ
is reflected in others
is reported in the Book
is imagined in faith

God reveals God

Search

Search for joy and find despair
Search for peace and find war
Search for life and find death
Search for forgiveness and find unforgiving
Search for truth and find the unknowns grow

Search for God and find All

Search for God

Search for God in worship and find the Church
Search for God in the Church and find worship
Search for God in the Book and find words
Search for God in words and find the Book
Search for God in others and find faith
Search for God in faith and find others

Search for God in you and find God

God Speaks

God can be easily silenced;
missed altogether;
talked over;
ignored completely;
God speaks softly.

The unanswered question

Why Me
How could I ever earn this meal
ever measure up
Why would God love me so much
God's Love is Unbelievable yet Undeniable

God

Diluted by mans faith
Filtered by mans words
Limited by mans logic
God must be experienced

God Gives

God did not sacrifice his son
Christ did not die for us
Christ lived for us
God offers you the same

God Loves Me

It appears that God loves others more.
God may in fact love others more.
Gods loves me enough that I may share at will.
I could not ask for more.
I love you.

God loves you

Merry Christmas

Christ can be born again.
Christ can live again.
Christ can be resurrected again.
All can happen in us each day.

Our last Day

If we live our life, our last day,
be it today or years from now.
We will
leave something undone;
some experiences never started;
leave someone without proper thanks;
be separated from love ones.
All to be rectified in time
as a spirit without the body.

God's Word

God's word has been filtered with time,
shaded by the faith of believers,
altered by translations;
Been used by the evil;
available directly form God

God's Love

Faith not feeling
Feeling but not knowing
Knowing but not understanding
Understanding but not absolute
Absolute not Faith

Sharing God's Love

God's love once shared
Binds you and God
You and Others
Others and You
You and ME

I Know

I Know
I do not understand
I Know
I can not explain
I Know
I find it hard to believe
Yet I Know

God's Word

God's word requires study
God's word serves
God's word is faith
God's word is true

God's word and God are absolute when
He speaks to you.

Gods Way

Known forever but never expected
Life's constant always ignored
Gods promise to all
The door to God
it is Gods way

God's Promise

God's gifts are
Knowing not Knowledge
Presence not Faith
Life not Death
God's Way
God's Promise

Gods, Promise

God never promised you that
you would understand.

God never promised you
there would not be pain.

God's promise is that
he would be with you.

God promise is life separated
by a transcending death.

Faith

God's love does not exclude the child
or the child like mind.
If your faith is based or more
It is your faith

Could God ?

Could God have created the universe,
yet meet me in spirit?
Could God be that Great
and love me?

Could God Know everything,
yet meet me in spirit
Could God know me
and love me?

I only know the presence
I only know the love

Answers

How could the answer
not answer all

The answer is
Greater than Man

Forgive me

If I seek my rewards
If I seek your rewards

Help me live the life given
Help me know your will

Everlasting

Life as given is everlasting
Some end it in life
Some end it at death

Life

There is no need for faith when
You know God has faith in you.

There is no need to believe when
You know God believes in you.

Dear God

God I would love you if you give me life.
I have already promised you that!

I would have great joy if you were with me.
I have been with you always!

God I will worship you.
I never asked for that!

God I would die for you.
I have already arranged for that!

God I accept Christ as you.
I love you

What Ever happens

What ever happens you will be OK

If you have your heart broken
Everyone has endured that

If you feel alone
All have felt that

If you die of cancer
Millions have endured that

If God Loves you
Nothing else matters

Pain

To avoid pain, never love
To avoid uncaring never care
To avoid being misunderstood never smile
To avoid life, never, never love God

The Beautiful Soul

A soul is what's given;
Is corrupted by the world;
Is eventually what you make it;
Yours is beautiful

Gods Blessings

We Pray as though we can control God's Blessings
We act as though we deserve God's Blessings
We work to insure we receive God's Blessings
We will never understand God's Blessings,
For sometimes pain is his blessing.

The Miracle

Man rejects his faith and accepts God
God gives his Love

Man rejects his past
God grants his Grace

Man rejects his nature
God accepts man

Man loses his life
God saves him

Man rejects God
It starts all over

The miracle is not God
God is absolute

The miracle is not God's actions
The miracle is God loves Man

A Miracle

Heart
Gods Love

Mind
Gods Grace

Soul
God

The Church

A mosaic of souls
Joined by God's love
Linked to the past
Connected to the future
Souls preserved for eternity
In God's Love

Reunion

A Soul deposited with God
Is nurtured by God
Preserved by God's love
and
Awaits the reunion

Woody

Accept Me, Accept my God

Honor Me, Honor my God

Love Me, Love my God

My

God is Love

God is More

Man's mind limits God
God must be more than mans limits.

Man's faith restricts God.
God must be more than mans faith.

God is More
God is Love

What would Jesus Do

Did Jesus accept the Scribes and Pharisees
for their knowledge of the Old Testament?

Does Jesus accept you
for your knowledge of the New Testament?

Did Jesus Love the Scribes and Pharisees
for their love of THE LAW?

Does Jesus love you
For your love of THE LAW?

Accept him

Did He raise the dead?
Is he the Father?

Did he heal the sick?
Is he the Son?

Did he walk on water?
Is he the Holy Ghost?

Know you will never understand and accept him.
Know you need not understand for him to accept You

Man's Faith in God

Mans faith can be with Gods presence
Man can almost become Jesus.

Mans faith can be without Gods presence.
Man can become God and do the most evil things.

Enough

I do not always know God's will
The future is uncertain
I can not find new meaning in the Verses
God's presence is enough
And more than I deserve

Salvation

God's law unlivable
God's presence
God's law unbreakable

Fate

Is there one alive who did not blame God for his Fate?
Is there one alive with God's presence' who does not
Thank God for his Fate?

The Law

Love God, love your neighbor

With God's presence

You can forgive yourself!
You can forgive your neighbor!
You can forgive God!

If Jesus came today would he

Heal the sick
Attend a gospel singing
Preach the Bible
Drink wine with his chosen
Appoint committees
Organize a Bible Study group
Attend Church
Lecture the Sinners
Build bigger Churches
Drive a Car
Feed the Hungry

Real

Abraham knew the absolute I know
Paul described it differently than I would
David said it more beautifully than I could
John saw the absolute I see
I know all have experienced what I have, but
all are different as my experience is different
As I am different

Knowing

Abraham, Paul, David and John
Were as human as you
God can be as absolute to you
as he was to them.

My Faith

My faith was my rock
My faith was my salvation
My faith was my path
My faith was my joy
I rejected my faith,
Accepted Jesus as the Son of God
And was born again.

The Absolute

You are the absolute
until you accept God.
When God accepts you
God is the Absolute.

Everything else is faith

Remember Me

Will Paul's Faith Suffice?
Will the Church's Faith Suffice?
Will your Faith Suffice?
He accepted Christ and saw paradise that day.

Was it his knowledge of theology?
Was it his knowledge of the Word yet to be written?
Was it his good deeds?
He accepted Christ and saw paradise that day.

God and You

The mind cannot prove God.
Faith cannot predict God.
The soul can accept God.
If not all, that is the beginning of life.

Your Sin

Thoughts which push God away.
Actions that separate's you from God
Punishment to live without God

Sin

God in the form of Jesus
    forgave the crucifers
        Will he
forgive those who do not believe?
        Will he
forgive those who condemn
    those who do not believe?
Will he forgive those who never hear of him?

Evolution

Is God's love an emotion ?
Is God's presence faith ?
Is a rock a vacuum ?
Is a sunrise evolution ?

Mans Evolution

A child matures
A man becomes a child
Mans faith evolves
The absolute is God

The Gift of Knowing

Time for hellos.
Time for goodbys.
Time for "Thanks".
Time for "I will miss you".
Time for acceptance of God
ALL Blessings some never have.

God's Greatest Gift

The unimportant is no longer Important.
The unknown is known.
The rituals lose their meaning.
It is final preparation for THE life.

Jesus Wept

Jesus Wept
Not for death
Not for life
For not accepting life
For not accepting God

I Think and Pray

I Think and Pray
I Think and Pray
I Think and Pray
I Think and Pray

Whys

The mind answers some
The heart answers some
The soul answers some
Faith answers some
God is the answer to all

God's answer is absolute

God's Answer

I Love you
Everything else will pass

Never and Forever

Your Mind cannot understand God
Your Faith cannot reach God
Your Heart cannot summon God
Your Soul cannot capture God
Your feelings are not God's Presence
Accept Jesus
And God will embrace you forever

God is love and pain

With God's love and presence
You feel great Joy and another's sorrow
You feel contentment and another's need
You feel great peace and another's torment

You feel concerned at another's condition

May you know the love and pain

Life is available by God's Touch

Birth
The beginning of life
Life
Death
Life

Accept
Welcome God's Touch

God's word is available

Unshaped by Faith
Unaltered by translation
Unsanctioned by the Church
Unqualified by others

Directly from God

I know all

Faith escapes me
Belief is beyond me
Explanation is missing

I know God's Presence
I know all

God's Gift

Beyond Faith
Beyond Belief
Beyond Explanation
Beyond life

God's Presence

Faith and Knowledge

Hope allows you to think God Loves you

Emotion allows you to feel God loves you

Faith allows you to believe God loves you

God allows you to know God loves you

Those who accept God

Suffer
Question
Endure
Die
Know God Loves Them

It is more than I can believe

A God who spoke to me;
A God who stood at my shoulder;
It is more than I can believe.
Yet It is something I know.

A God who knows me;
A God that loves me;
It is more than I can believe.
Yet He is absolute.

Possessions

Grace in not a condition to be earned.
Love is not a state to be maximized
Forgiveness is not an objective to be won.
Life is not to be rationed.
They are God's gift to be shared.

To Know

Your gift of Knowing is everything.
Why can't I find the words?
Why can't I share it with others?

Seek God

Search with your Heart.
Reject your feelings.
Search with your Mind.
Reject your conclusions.
Search with your Soul.
Reject your Faith.
He can find you.

Faith

Your Faith in Faith
Is not Faith in God

Your Faith in God
Is not God

<u>God IS</u>
Just Accept Him

God is

God is in Christ

God is in me

God is in you

If not in us
God is
Within our reach

I believe

I believe in Jesus
I believe he is the son of God
I believe in the trinity
I believe in the Church
I believe …
The good news is
God loves me, not my faith

God Loves You

Not Your prayers
Not Your beliefs
Not Your actions
Not Your faith

God loves you

All we have

All we have is God
If we accept him

All we have is God's Gifts
If we accept them

God's Gifts

Limited Body
Limited Faith
Limited Knowledge
Unlimited Love
Gifts only when accepted
Gifts only when shared

When God Is

When one's God is vengeful
One God is better than another

When one's God is Faith
One God is as good as another

When one's God is Love
One's God is another's

Faith Separates and Joins

God was with us at birth
We Think
We Reason
We Believe
Our faith separates us from God
Our Acceptance reunites us to God

My Debt

Not to the cross
Nor the crucifixion
Not the past
Nor the future
For the presence
For the love

Your Debt

Not to the cross
Nor the crucifixion
Not the past
Nor the future
For the presence
For the love

The only Sin

Against God
Against your neighbor
Against your loved ones

Is against yourself

The Gap

The Gap between you and God
Grows with your actions
Widens with your beliefs
Narrows with your acceptance
Closed by GOD
It is just a matter of Time

DEATH

Time not lived
Things not completed
Love not expressed
All before the
One on One Meeting
with a loving God

One on One Meeting
with a loving God

Acceptance of death
Acceptance of Christ

It is the beginning of life
It is beyond your understanding.

The Beautiful Soul

Leads by following.

Depth of example.

Shouts Quietly

Touches the heart by being

Beautiful

Barriers

The bible
The church
The pastor

Your faith
Your beliefs
Your logic

Things that Separates You and God
Anything You allow between
You and God
Nothing until you allow it

Man

The world is Logical
God must be logical
I am not always logical
God must not always be logical

The world loves
God must be loving
I do not always love
God must not always be loving

Parents

Is there a mother who does
not pray for her son

Did not Mary pray for Jesus

Is there a father who does not pray for his daughter

Care free

A birthing gasp, a mourning cry
A frown, A warm smile
A laugh. A sob
A broken heart, A heart felt joy

With God there are no care free days

Just You and God

You can be told about God
You can study God
You can learn God
You can reason God
You can grow in God
You can believe in God
You can have faith in God

You can know God
The rest is just faith

The church

You can love the world, that is our portion of it.
You can love all mankind if they are on our list
You can love the needy if you hate the rich
You can love God If you love him like us.

God Speaks to You

God spoke to Adam and Eve
Who did not know the Old or New

God spoke to Abraham
Who did not know the Old

God spoke to David
Who did not know the New

God speaks to all
Who listen
Accept and love

Church

Man is fatally flawed
The church is all men
The church is flawed
God is the only reliable witness to God

Turn to God

Turn to the pastor
They are men
Turn to the Church
They are men
Turn to the Bible
Even inspired they were men
Turn to Christ
He was part man
Turn to God
God is the only reliable
witness to God

Turn to God and your neighbor
That is all Christ asked of you

You Can Know

You can know the scriptures
You can know the faith
You can know the church
You can know the word
Reject all

You can know God if you accept Christ

You Know

You know a tree by its fruit
You know a man by his God
You know a Christian by his neighbor
You know God by his presence

Gods Presence

You can know the Word
You can know your Neighbor

You know God's Love
You Know God

Methodist

Love God
The one in our Constitution

Love your neighbor
They are in our Book of Discipline

Love our rituals
Collectively we are God

Forgive us

We study the Bible to find an out
How to avoid the harsh truth

We attend church
to avoid a neighbor

We love those who help us
Those who don't are not Godly

Still

We attend the church
We praise our faith
We love the far away poor
We ignore our neighbor who can not help us
We feel good about ourselves
We help our friends who do not need us
We love God for what we want

Still we are forgiven

YOU CAN

You can believe in Abraham and your faith can make you a Jew

You can believe in Abraham and your faith can make you a Moslem

You can believe in Abraham and your faith can make
you one of a hundred types of Christians

You can believe in Christ and your faith can make
you one of a hundred types of Christians

You can accept Christ and be loved by God
Your heart, mind and soul will be filled with God's love

Man builds towers to God

Some use bricks
Others use faith

Some use rocks
Others use song

Some use good deeds
Others use theology

Some use Poetry
Some Bible Study

All fail as man cannot reach God
God reaches man when invited
When accepted

You Know

YOU KNOW A TREE BY ITS FRUIT
YOU KNOW A MAN BY HIS GOD
YOU KNOW A CHRISTIAN BY HIS NEIGHBOR
YOU KNOW GOD BY HIS PRESENCE
INVITE AND ACCEPT GOD

GOD'S FAITH

GOD HAS FAITH IN YOU
GOD BELIEVES IN YOU
GOD'S WORD IS AVAILABLE
DIRECTLY FROM GOD, ASK GOD
GOD IS THE OMLY RELIABLE
WITHNESS TO GOD

Scribes and Pharisees

If you need a neighbor to finance your ministry
You no not have a ministry
If you minister to one neighbor,
At the expense of another.
You do not have a Neighbor.
You are a Scribe and Pharisee

YOU CAN

You can believe in Abraham and your faith can make you a Jew

You can believe in Abraham and your faith can make you a Moslem

You can believe in Abraham and your faith can
make you one of many types of Christians

You can believe in Christ and your faith can make
you one of many types of Christians

You can accept Christ and be loved by God
Your Heart, mind and soul will be filled with God's love

Only Scribes and Pharisees know more

Man builds towers to God

Some use bricks
Others use faith

Some use rocks
Others use song

Some use good deeds
Others use theology

Some use Poetry
Some Bible Study

Some use Greek
Others use Hebrew

All fail as man cannot reach God
God reaches man when invited
When accepted

Scribes and Pharisees

Pick their Neighbors
Pick their Book, Chapter, and Verse
Pick those to love
Pick their Faith
And pick their God
And always build the house for Christ he rejected

YOU CAN

Earn a Title, Earn a position
Earn a promotion, Earn knowledge
Earn a Living. Join a church
Build a church
God builds <u>The CHURCH</u>
Within
The souls of Men
You must accept <u>The CHURCH</u>
As you accept Christ

God's Love

Christ has already come
When you have God's love.
God has already judged
when you have God's love.
Death is a door not the end
when you have God's love.
The end of time has come
when you have God's love.

My Song, My Sermon, My Prayer

God is greater than the Church,
Pray for me.
God is greater than the Bible, Pray for me,
Pray for me.
God is greater than Jesus, Prayer for me,
Pray for me.
God is greater than the accepted God,
Pray for me,
God is the only absolute, I pray for You,
I pray for you.

With your acceptance of Christ
God speaks without sound.
God's presence fills the heart,
the mind, the soul.

Scribes and Pharisees

What would Jesus Do

He would recognize
The changes in man
The changes in knowledge
The changes in language
The changes in priorities
The changes in Faiths
The new needs of man

WHY

I can ask questions I cannot answer
I can know things I cannot explain
I can experience things I cannot understand
God made me human not God
Thank You God

God Is

God cannot be judged by fate.
God cannot be judged by the action of believers.
God cannot be judged.
God is not belief.
God is.

Everything else pales

In the belly of a whale.
In the arms of a mob.
In the embrace of cancer.
God loves you.

Everything else is faith.
Everything else passes.

Everything else pales.

Scribes and Pharisees

The Books were written by scribes
They were collected by Constantine
They were assembled by the Bishops
Declared Holy by a council
Interpreted by Pharisees
All imperfect Men

Still

GOD is Love
God's Word is Love
Man's word is man's
Still we are forgiven

Still in a Wilderness

Preachers who find new meaning in the word

Prophets who can reveal the future

Anyone who has his own faith.

Prefers his version of the Bible

Prefers his Faith over others

God's answer is Love

Life is a wilderness

Where?
When?
How?
You don't say?
Do you really believe that?

Gods answer is Love

We study the Bible to find a way out
How to avoid the harsh truth

We attend church
To avoid a neighbor in need

We love those who help us
Those who don't, are not Real Christens

Still

We attend the church
We praise our faith
We love the far away poor
We ignore our neighbor who can not help us
We feel good about ourselves
We help our friends who do not need us
We love God for what we want
Still we are forgiven

God's love is the only absolute

You have no Faith!

You must have Faith!

You must have a Faith

You must have the Faith

You must have My Faith

You must have Our Faith

You must have a Named Faith

When you accept any you have turned away from God

Faith defined is not Faith

God's Failures

God is great but could be greater.

He could have eliminated my pain.
He could have made me smarter.
He could have made me better

He could have made me God.

When you are human; it is all too easy to be God.

Questions and Answers

God created me to ask questions I cannot answer.
It must be the effort not the results, which is important.
It must be the trip, not the destination.
It must be the question, not the answer.
God lives in me.
It must be the results not the effort that is important.
It must be the destination, not the trip.
It must be the answer, not the question.

It is for God not me.
It is human for me to try.

God reveals God

God is mirrored in Christ
Is reflected in others
Is reported in the Book
Is imagined in faith

God reveals God

Search

Search for joy and find despair
Search for peace and find war
Search for life and find death
Search for forgiveness and find the unforgiving
Search for truth and find the unknowns grow

Search for God and find LOVE

Scribes and Pharisees

Praise God to demonstrate their Faith
Love Christ to earn a Life
Preach the Bible to demonstrate Their Faith
Separate you from "sinners" To obtain your respect
Promote the Church to enhance their career
Learn to Preach
Pray for all, Visit the sick
And memorize your name

A Minister

Loves God
And his neighbor

You Can

You can worship your faith and love yourself.
You can love the Word and love yourself
You can accept God and be loved by God
You can love others

Your Ego is your Faith
Your Faith is your Ego

Allows you to believe you are better than others
know more than others
feel more than others
desire the company of others
God's presence insures you love others

Thanks God

Your disciples
Your book
Our teachers
Our preachers
Our ministers
Even our children
All now know more about you than Christ

Feel Good

If you believe you are good you are good
If you believe you are useful you are useful
If you feel you are loved you are loved
If you feel and accept a neighbors pain
You are loved by God

God Gives Life

God gives life with options.
Each life must choose life each Day.
Each life must choose life after death.
God gives life forever.

Creation

A God created by Man
Will speak only to
Day care employees
Sunday school teachers
Deacons
Lay Speakers
Pastors
Ministers
Scribes
Prarisees
Theologian
Ministers
Bishops
Popes
Saints

The God who created man
Will speak to
You
Any Man
Any Woman
Any child

Trilogy

A creation of man?
An object of Faith?
A creation of Theology?
A splitting of hairs?

Does it matter.

God is

Man Creates His Own God

From his needs
From his wants
From his desires

Adjectives piled high

In Words
In song
In worship

In his personal Faith
In his Church's Faith
In his Religion's Faith

GOD IS

Not faith

The First Coming

My Salvation

Since the age of six I have had many questions about God that no one could answer. In my early twenty's I decided that both Plato and Aristotle were right and both wrong. They believed that the world was in fact a giant pyramid and in order to understand the world and God. You must understand the pyramid and the order of the world. Plato believed you must start with God who was at the top of the pyramid and with logic work your way down. He believed man was the highest creation of God as he made all animals and plant for man's use, therefore he loved man. If you hear anything about Plato today it is the phrase plutonic love" or pure love.

Aristotle on the other hand believed in the pyramid but that logic required that in order to understand God you must understand his creation. He believed that man must start at the bottom of the pyramid and work himself up to God. He is considered the father of Science.

From these; the present conflict between Science and Faith- Religion was born

I spent at least 40 years believing that If I pursued God with faith (Pluto's logic), and with logic (Aristotle's logic), I would eventually know more about God than any one else. I would understand Gods creations and purpose.

During those years I sensed that there was a higher being looking out for me. I at times sensed that the road I was on was a mistake and viewing those who went down that road never came back, the admission of wrong was too great a task for most people to accept. It was easier to change your beliefs that to admit to the mistaken road. I could never understand but every time I changed direction it proved with time I had made the right choice.

These experiences usually happened with unexpected delays and confusion as well as events that led to concern and questioning. Life has those moments and some times they extend for months and years.

The one that changed my life lasted for about 6 months. I had a job to go to Tunis in North Africa to teach some students in the operation of a truck refueler for aircraft. Training was in French and I was unique in the requirements.

The training was supposed to occur before the vehicles arrived in Tunis and this would have made it difficult to train them properly. I suggested the Training be delayed until the vehicles arrived. This led to at least 6 months of delay that usually was extended for a week or a few days at a time. I was wondering if it would every happen I just put my head down and toughed it out as I was sure that if I did so, eventually I would make it happen.

I finally got the go ahead for the trip and made the arrangements for a flight. A day before the flight the call came to delay again another week. I left the next morning and my wife notified them I had already left and would be there on time.

I arrived in Rome Italy a week early and debated where to spend the week. I had planned a trip to a small town in Germany where I was stationed 30 years before as a teenager. I decided to make that trip and see the countries in between. My schedule was not fixed and depended on moment to moment decisions. The only thing was that there was one town I felt I would never need to see again and did not plan to visit. The town was Trier Germany. This town is the oldest town in Europe and was once a Capital of the Northern Roman Empire and remains a small town today. I was sure there was nothing there that would interest me as I had lived 10 miles away for three years.

I discovered I could not take a train directly to the place I wanted to go and settled for a train to Trier. I arrived at 9 pm and was confronted with the situation of a celebration of the Robe. I was told by the station mister that there were no rooms left in town, rooms had been sold out for the festival for some time. I remembered what I liked least about Europe as they are all ways celebrating some obscure event that we never heard of. There was no train out of town, no rooms in town and the taxies were going home. The train station clerk approached and said there was in fact a room as another passenger did not arrive. I got the last taxi and made it to the address, paid the driver and he went home for the night. I hotel was dark with no lights and no one answered the bell.

I settled down beside the door sitting on my luggage and wondered if I slept here would I be disturbed. After about 10 minutes the lights came on and the hotel owner opened the door and gave me a room. He was fond of Americans and we talked about the town and the celebration of the Robe. Again I was not interested in specifics.

The next morning I traveled to the town I was stationed at 30 years before. I returned about 2 pm and found the little town of Trier completely filled with people. It was a Sunday and was not unusual for a small German town. I met an American Family and we talked for 30 minuets or so about the town. They were for the robe celebration but my mind was closed to the specifics.

I had revisited my youth and was eager to get on with my life and accomplish those goals which I had not accomplished and went to bed early.

I was up at 6:30 and the streets were empty. The sun was up as Germany is north of most of the US. As I was walking around the empty town I noticed an open door at a small chapel. I entered to find the chapel filled with mature women, all with heads bowed and in prayer. I saw a glass enclosed box displaying a robe at one side of the chapel. I decided that I must see what all the fuss was about. I approached the case and bowed to see the garment. I immediately noticed it simplicity. It was without any seams, collars or hems on the arms or bottom. I was wearing a knit shirt. I thought we can do that with a machine but this was done by hand. The garment was made with what appeared to be wool, the yarn was very large and appeared to be a heavy knitting thread. The color was dark dull orange and appeared to have the dark hair and black specks found in un-carded wool. I marveled at the skill of the person who made the garment and left.

I collected my luggage and arrived at the train about 8.30 am with a wait of about an hour. I thought there is nothing else for me to do but wait. After 15 minutes I was walking back and forth along the platform when I noticed a monk selling a small trinket. so I purchased one and was given a pamphlet. I returned to my luggage and placed both in a bag. I purchased it mainly for my wife, as she had spent some time in the town when she was young volunteer worker and may know what it was and would be interested.

After another 15 minutes I retrieved the pamphlet and read it. It turns out it was supposedly the Seamless Robe of Christ returned from Jerusalem by Helen the Mother of Constantine who made a very early pilgrimage to Jerusalem. She returned with the Robe and the Cross.

I had believed for 30 years that I must apply both faith and Science to understand God. At that time I arrived at the conclusion that neither my logic or faith would every allow me to understand God, That It was time to abandon both my logic and faith and just accept that He is real

In the middle of that thought and before the thought was finished I sensed the arrival of God from behind me and at my level. Love so engulfed me that there was love for everyone on the earth and everything on the earth. God silent words were "I am here just to tell you that I love you".

I found out later that the robe of Trier is only shown every 30 to 35 years. The time I saw it was not on the schedule of events. As there is no record of it, I conclude it was for the locals only and information about it was not revealed to the public. I believe against all odds that I was led to that door by many changes in my life by God. I believe he had arranged for other events that I ignored throughout my life.

Text: Dr. Franz Ronig, Professor

Trier Cathedral and the Holy Robe

The most precious relic in Trier Cathedral is the Holy Robe, the tunic of Christ. According to tradition, the Empress Dowager Helena brought the seamless robe of Christ to Trier. The Holy Robe is mentioned for the first time in the 11th century; the history of the Holy Robe is documented with certainty only from the 12th century, when it was removed from the west choir to the new altar in the east choir on May 1, 1196.

In 1512:

Opening of the high altar in the presence of Emperor Maximilian under Archbishop Richard of Greiffenklau and the first pilgrimage to the Holy Robe

Further Pilgrimages:

1513, 1514, 1515, 1516, 1517, 1524, 1538, 1545, 1655, 1810, 1844, 1891, 1933, 1959, 1996

Since the Cathedral renovation in 1974, the Holy Robe has been kept in its wooden shrine from 1891, lying under an air-conditioned glass shrine. The last great pilgrimage, in 1996, became a celebration of all the faithful, with its continuation in the annual Holy Robe Days. Only during the Holy Robe Days is the Holy Robe chapel accessible, but the garment cannot be viewed. The original state of the textile has altered because of past events and the unfavorable storage conditions, as repairs have frequently been made.´

The question of the genuineness ot the Holy Robe cannot not be answered with certainty. For the faithful, the symbolism is important: the relic signifies Jesus Christ Himself, His incarnation and the other events in His life up to the crucifixion and His death. The undivided and seamless garment is also a symbol of undivided Christianity and evokes the binding power of God, as ist expressed in the Trier pilgrim's prayer:

"Jesus Christ, Savior and Redeemer, have mercy on us and all the word. Be mindful of Thy Church and bring together what is diveded. Amen."

Text: Dr. Franz Ronig, Professor

God's Revelation

We live in a logical world
Logic will not reveal God
But
Neither will faith
God Reveals God

We do not understand our children

We do not understand our parents

We do not understand our grandparents

Some of us do understand

Every thought of Christ

Every thought of God

The end of the world

And more